MERRY CHRISTMAS!

a black and white baby book

ADAM HARRIS

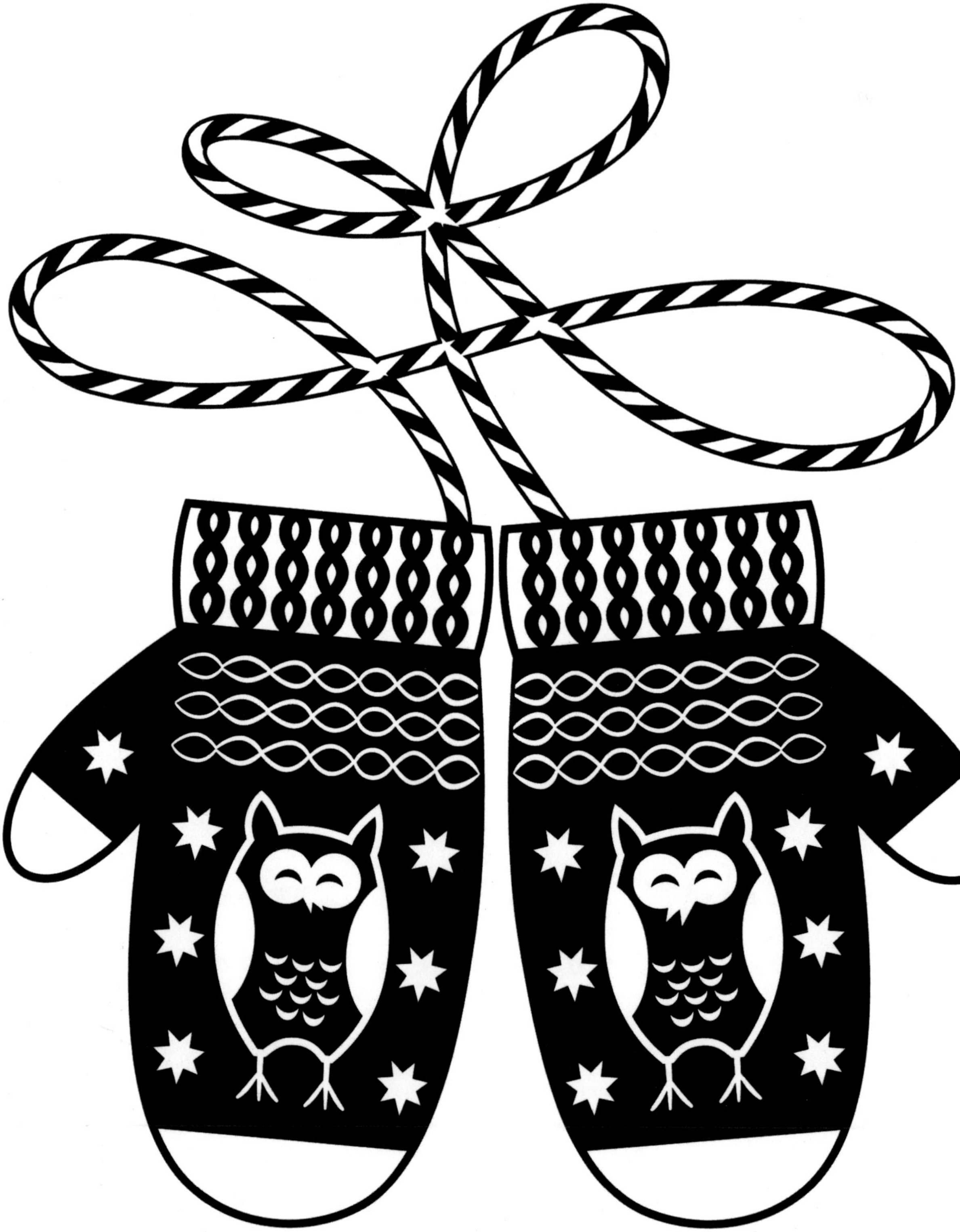

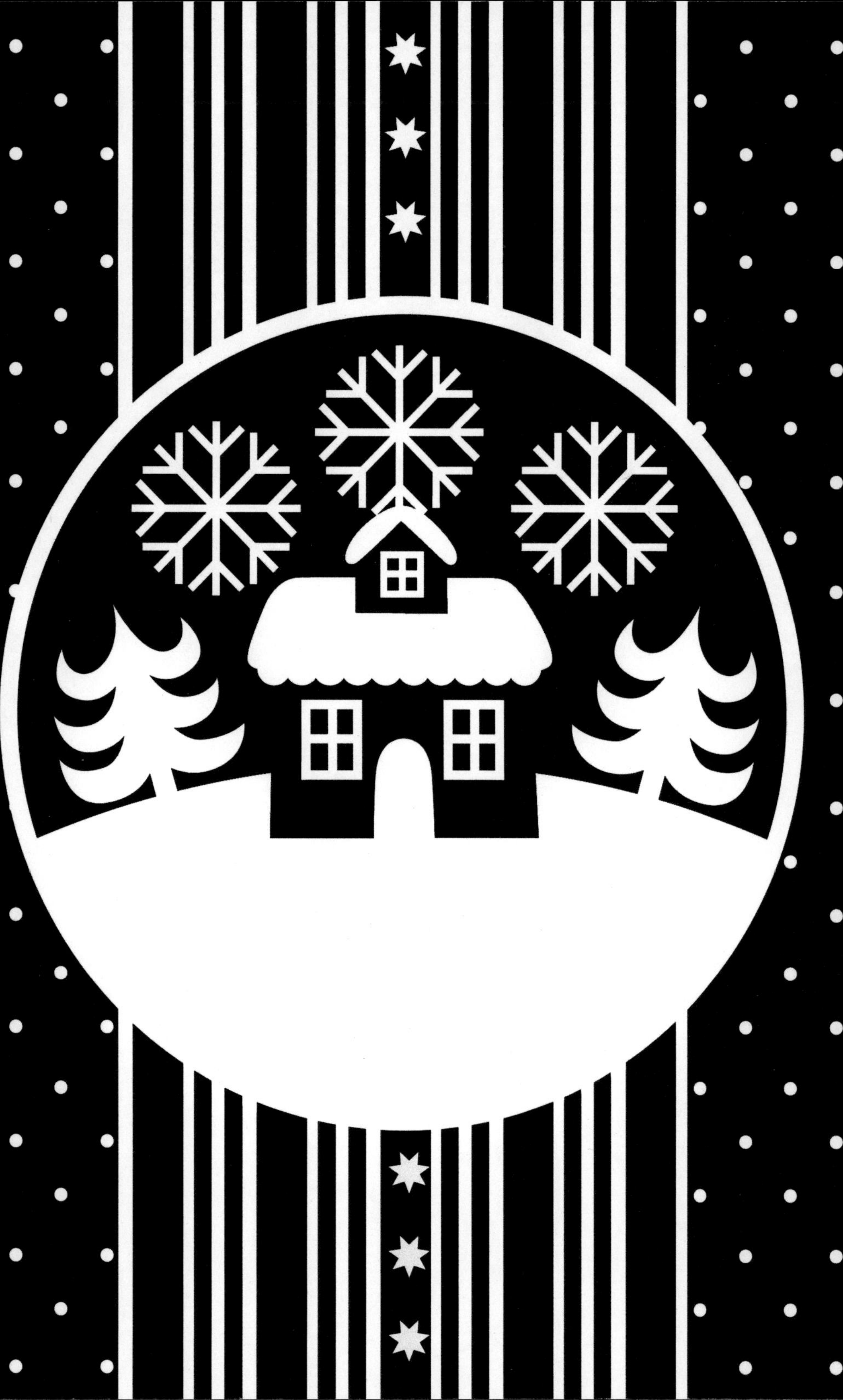

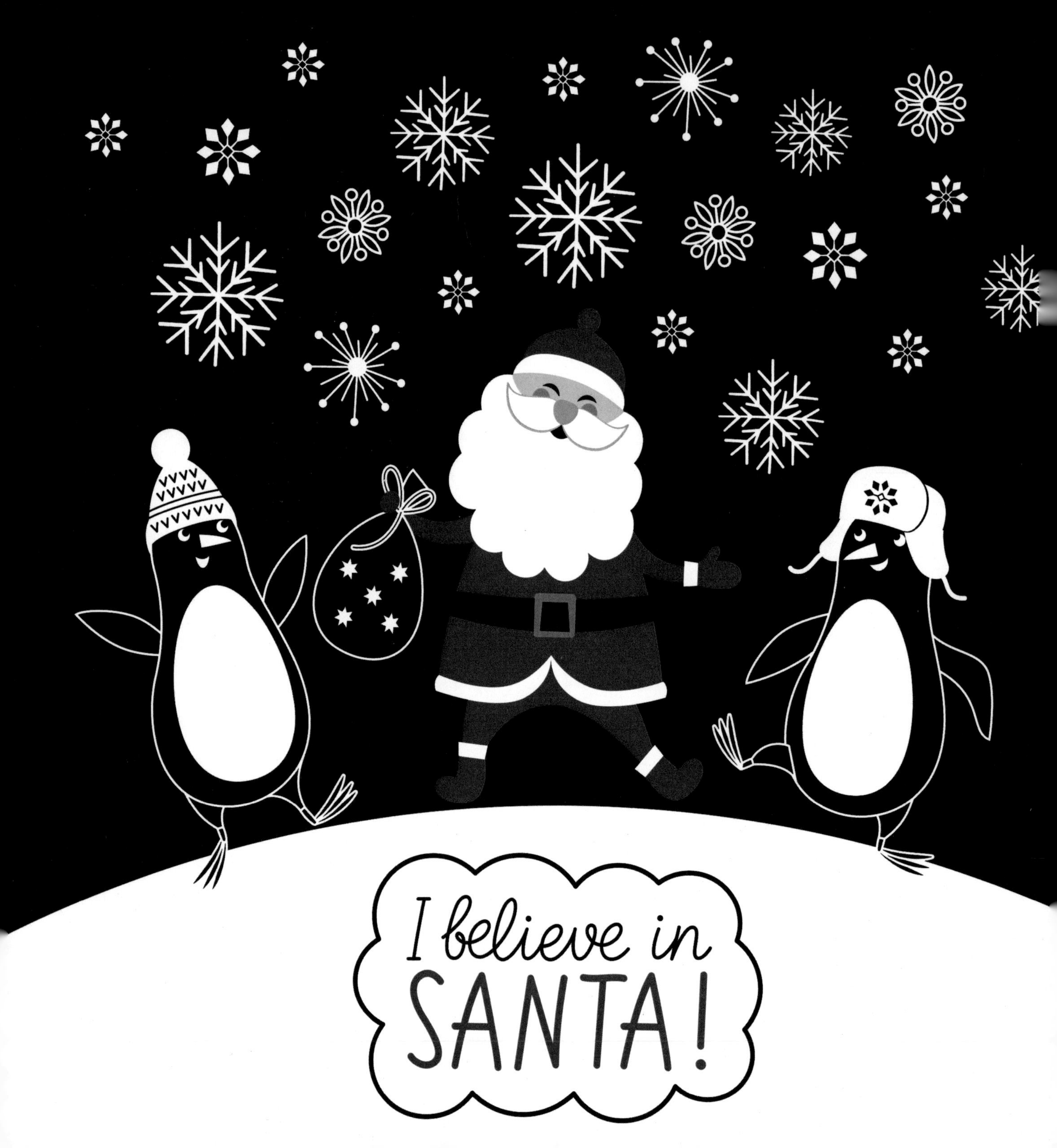
I believe in
SANTA!

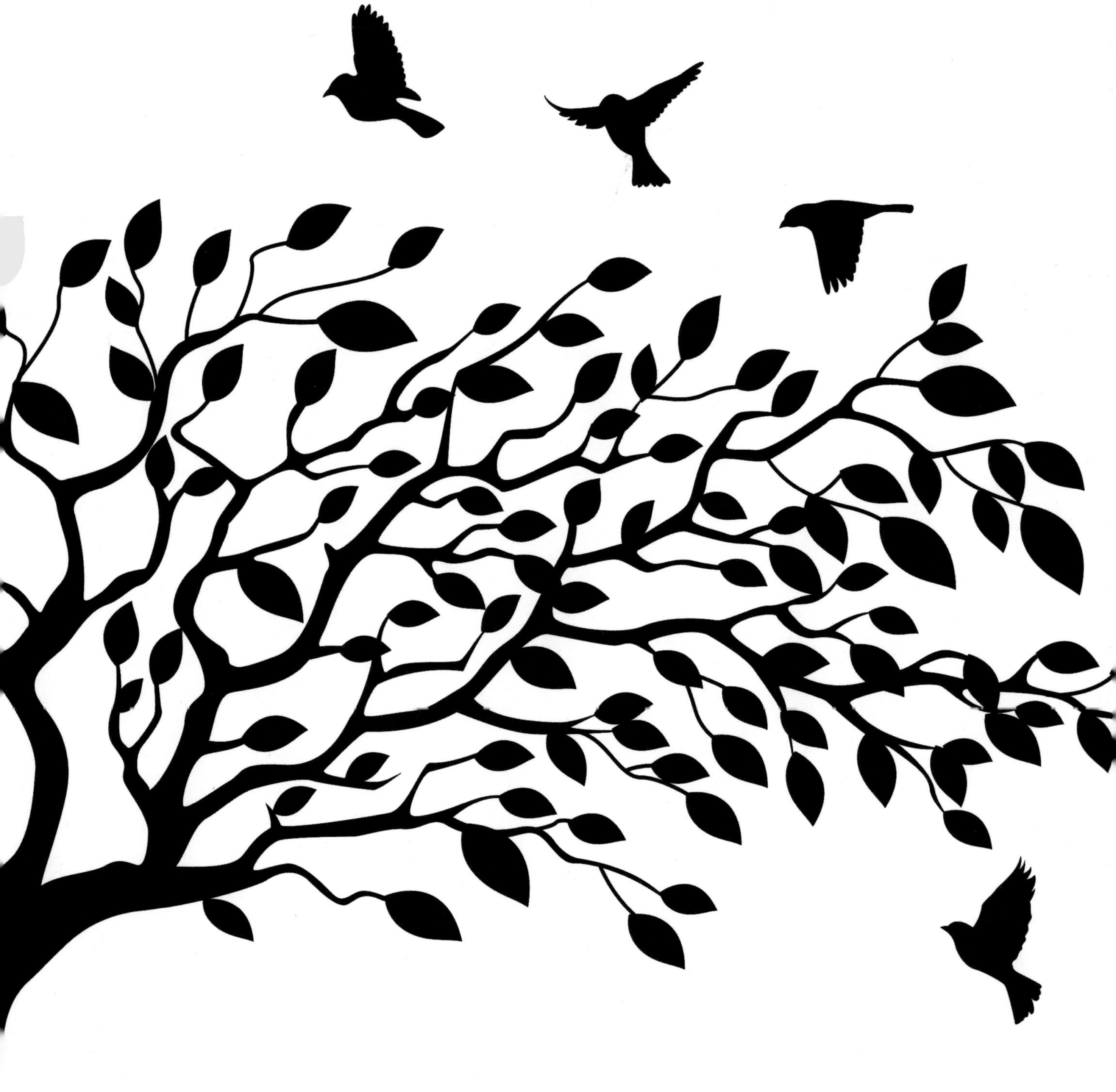

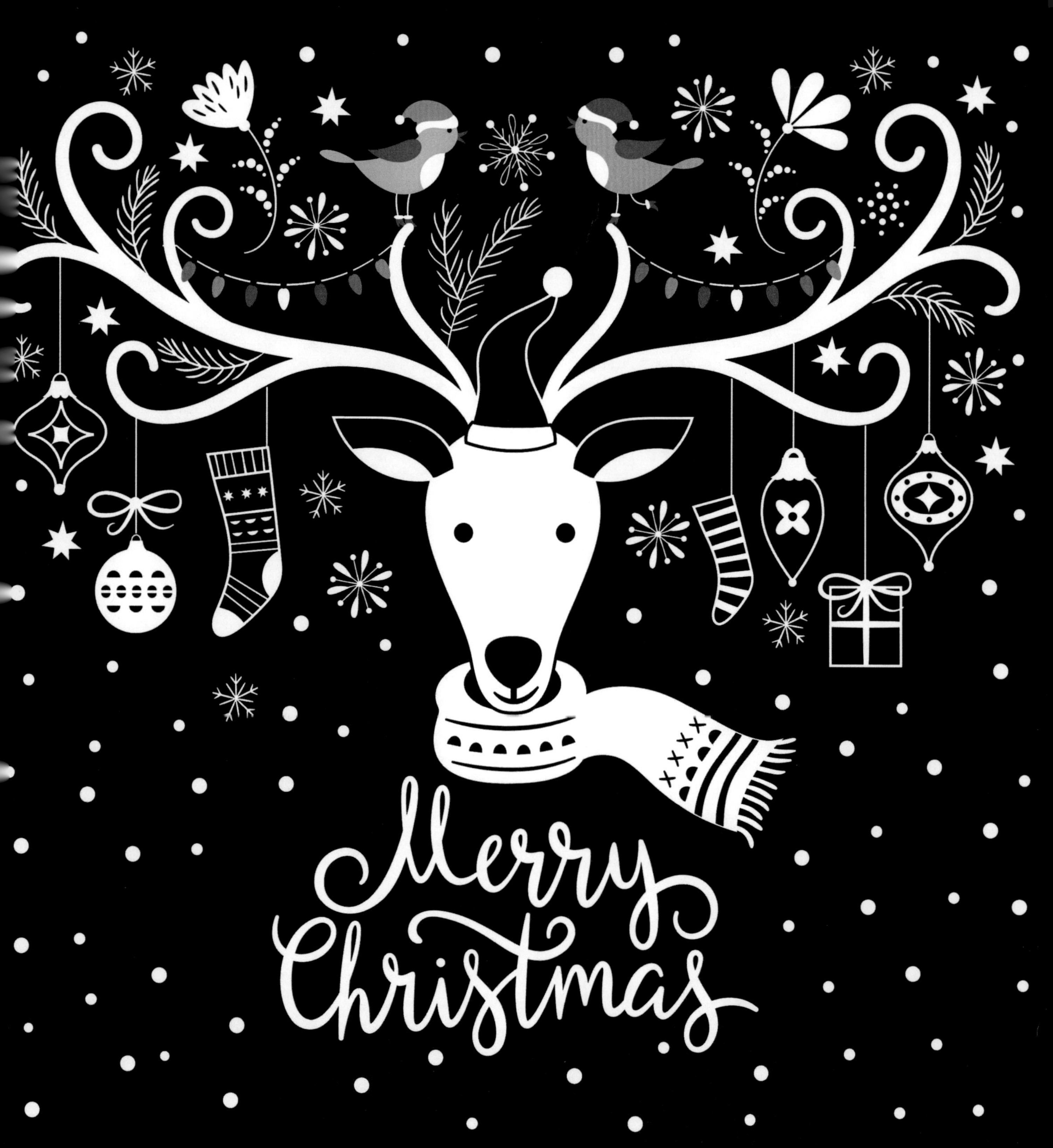
Merry Christmas

Oh DEER

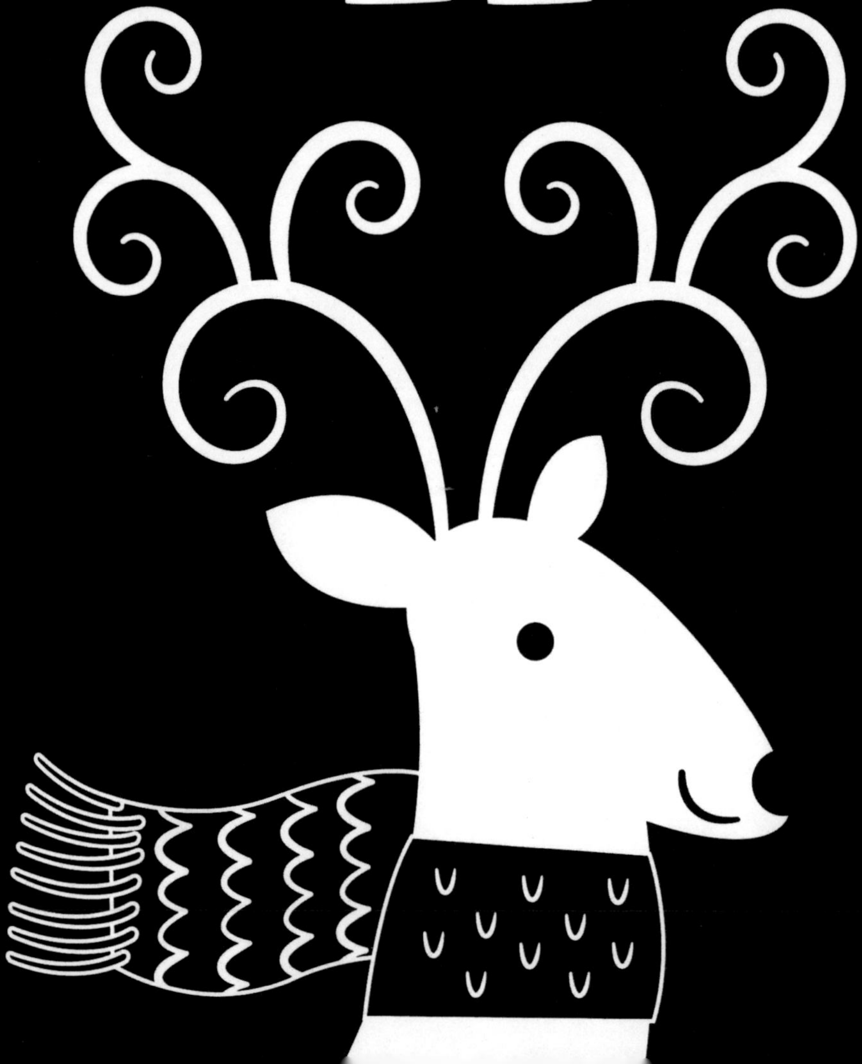

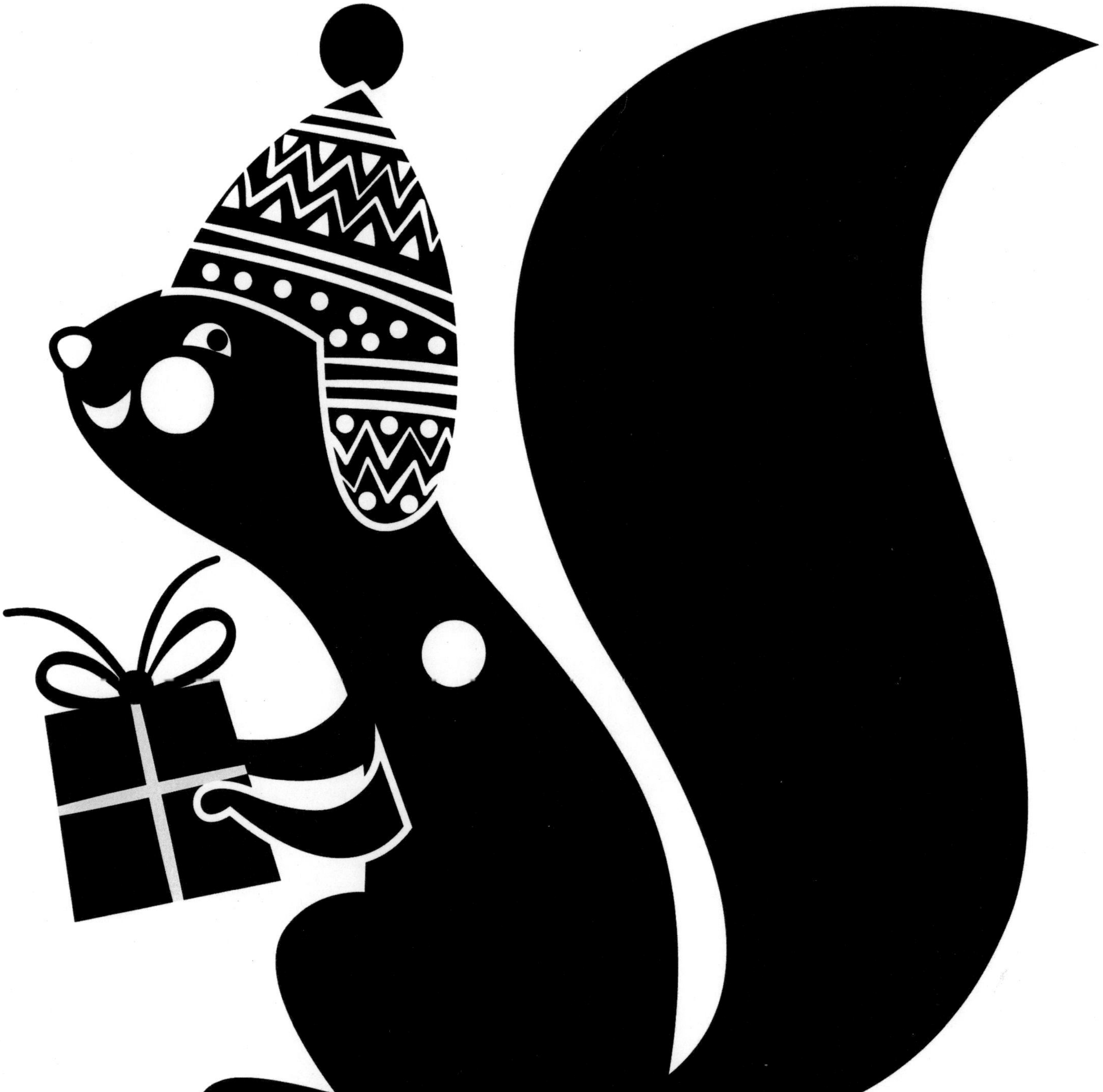

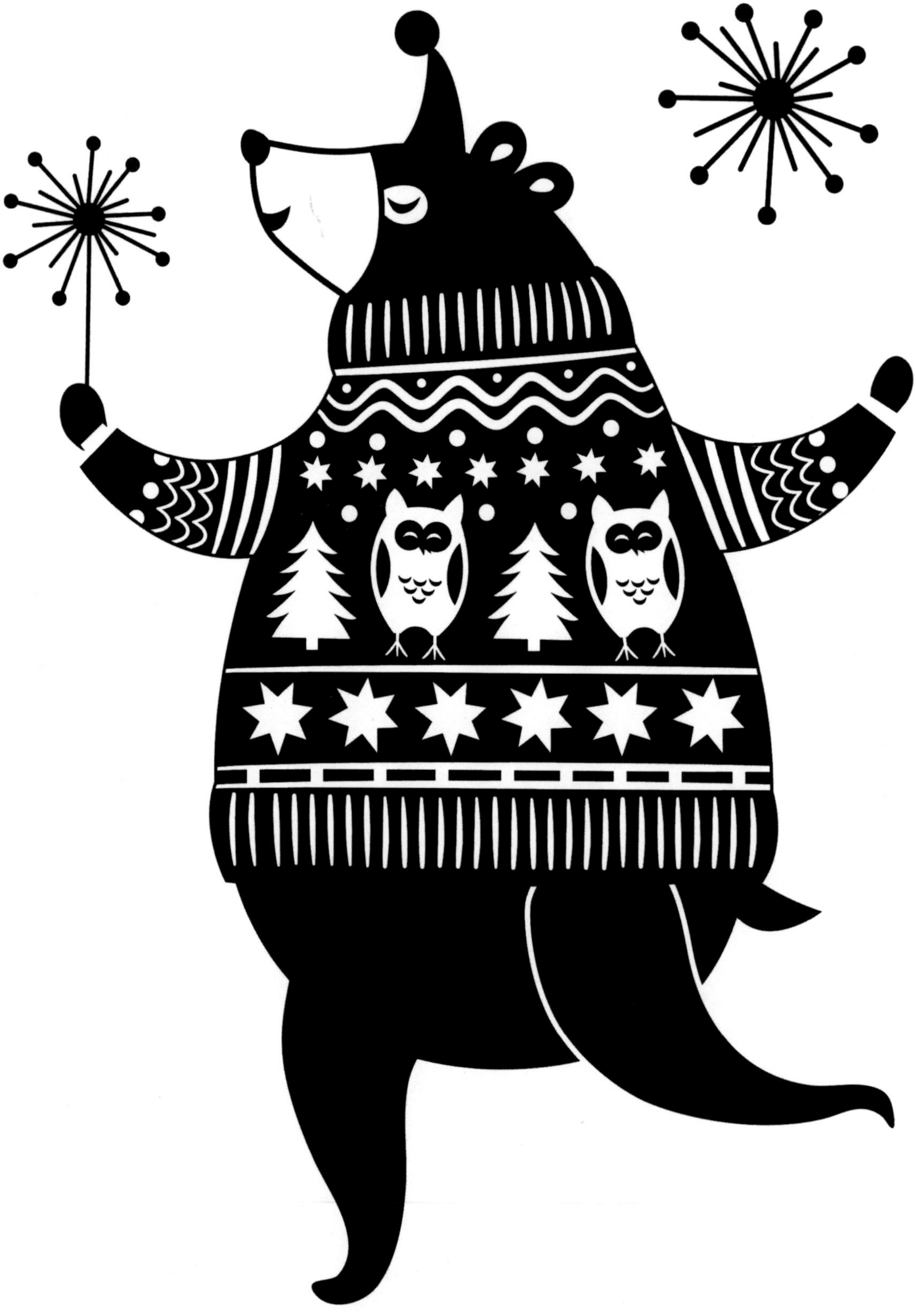

build a SNOW MAN

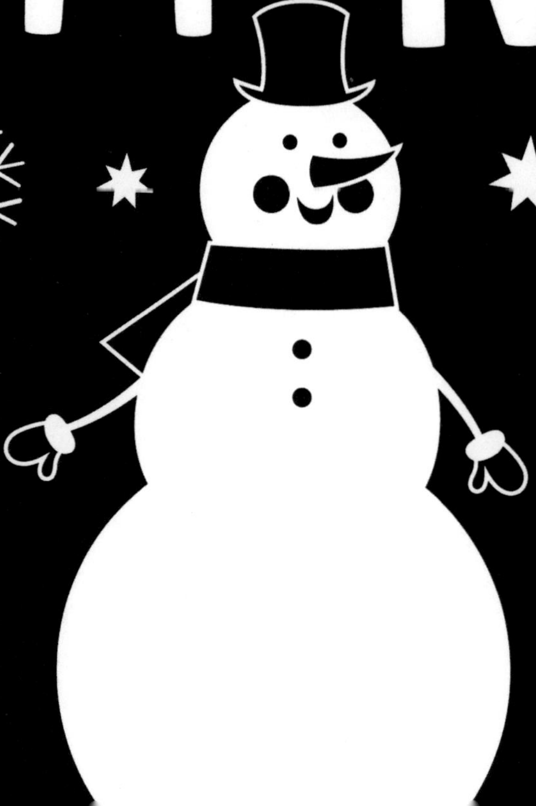

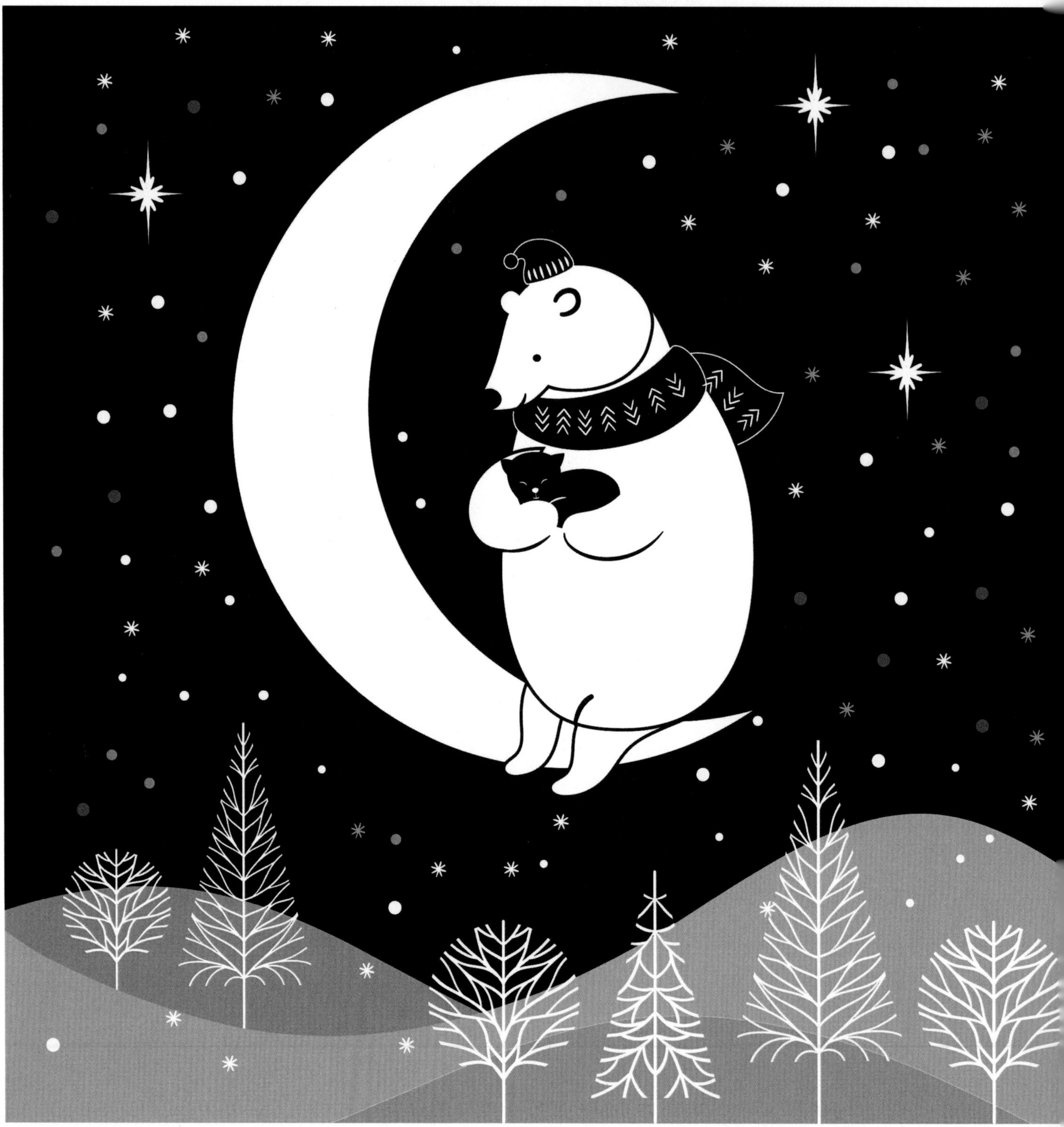

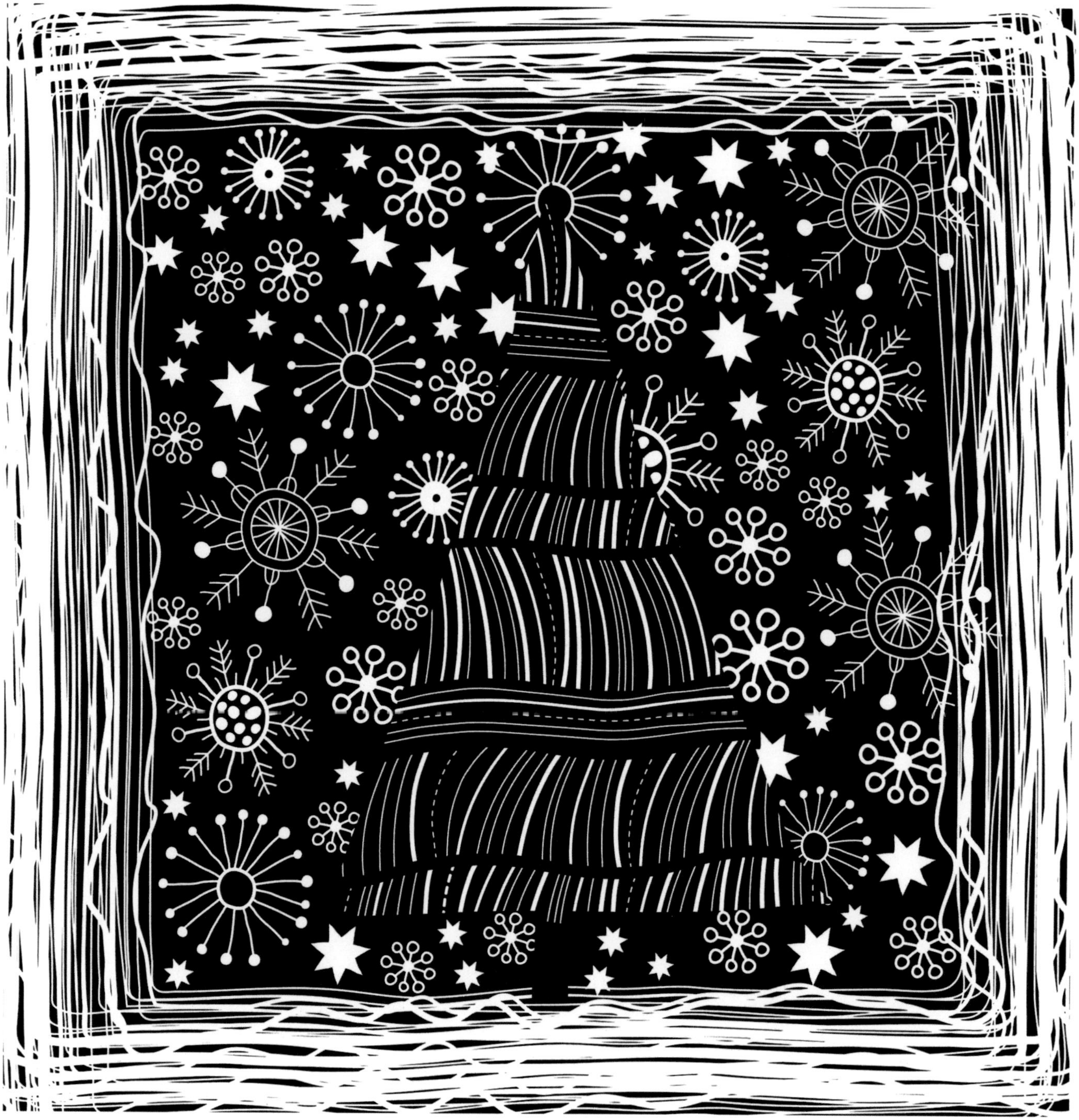

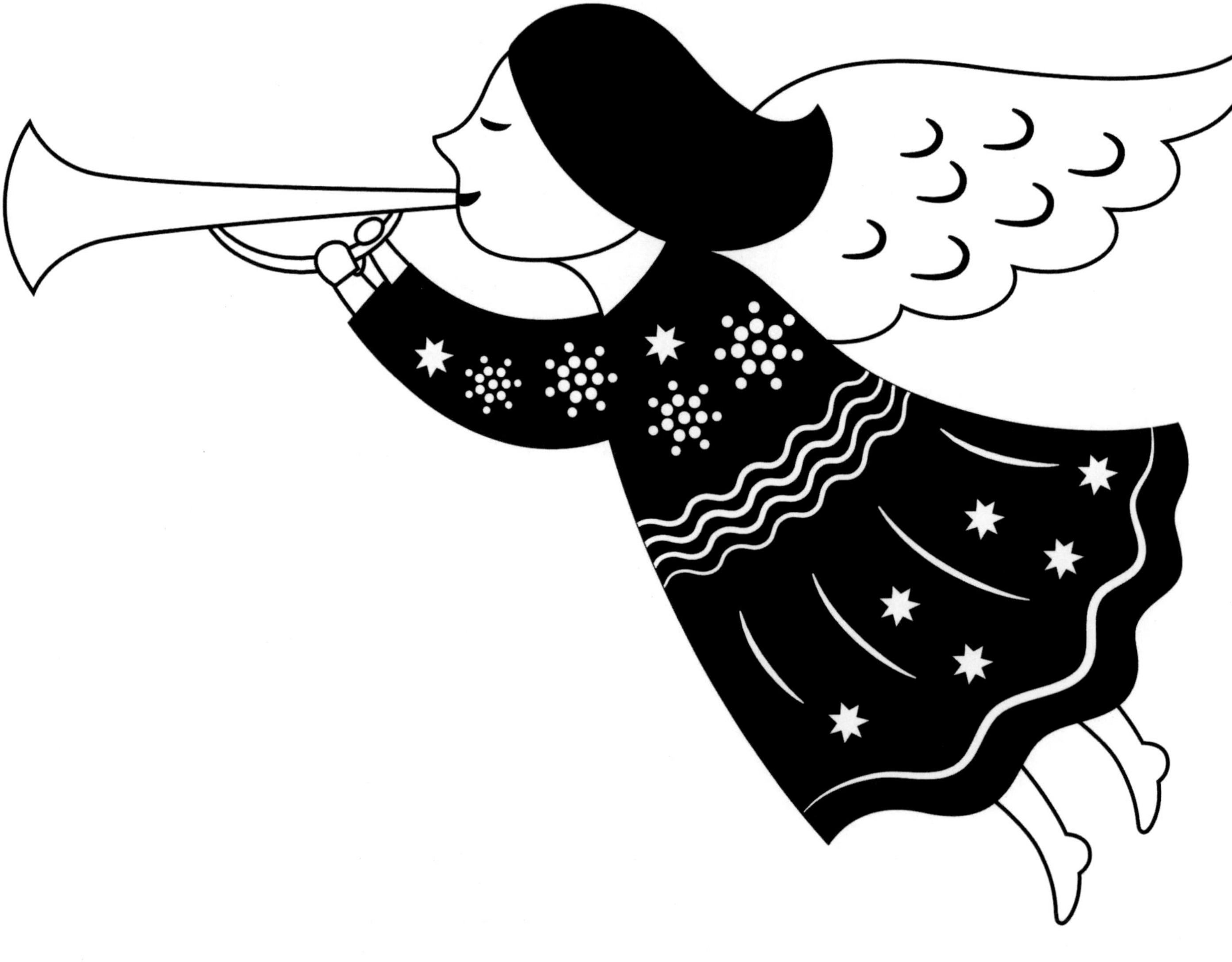

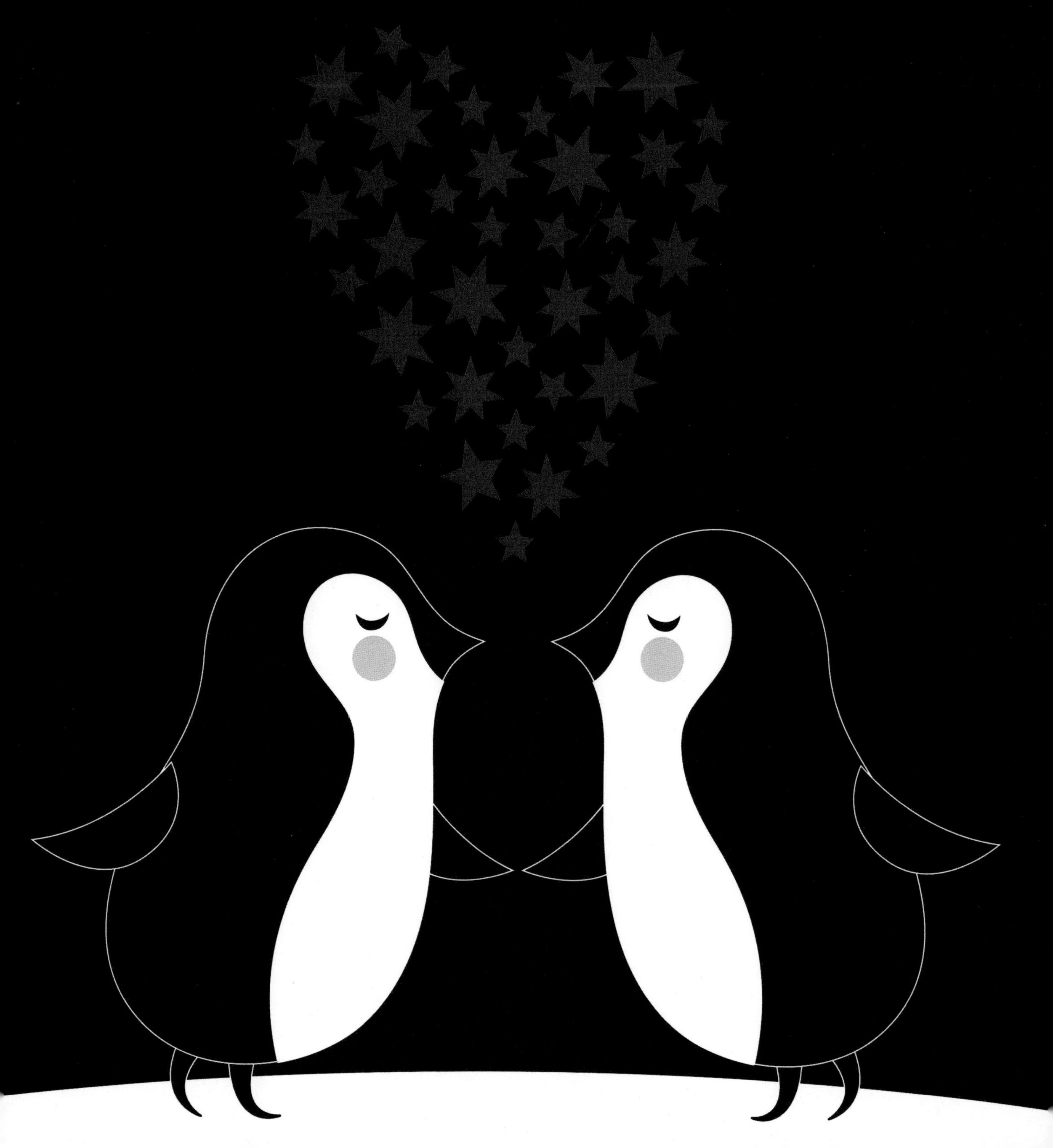

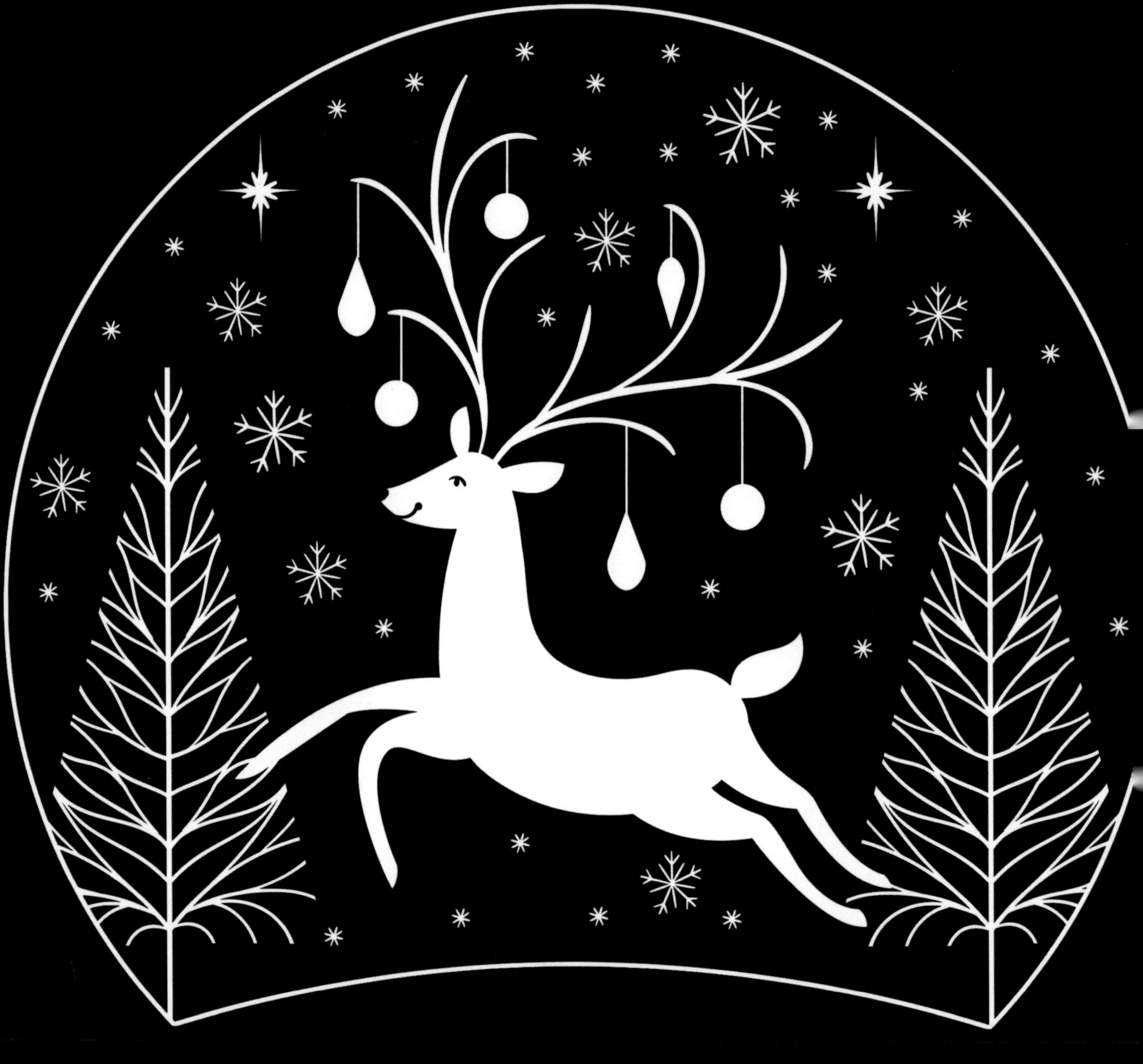

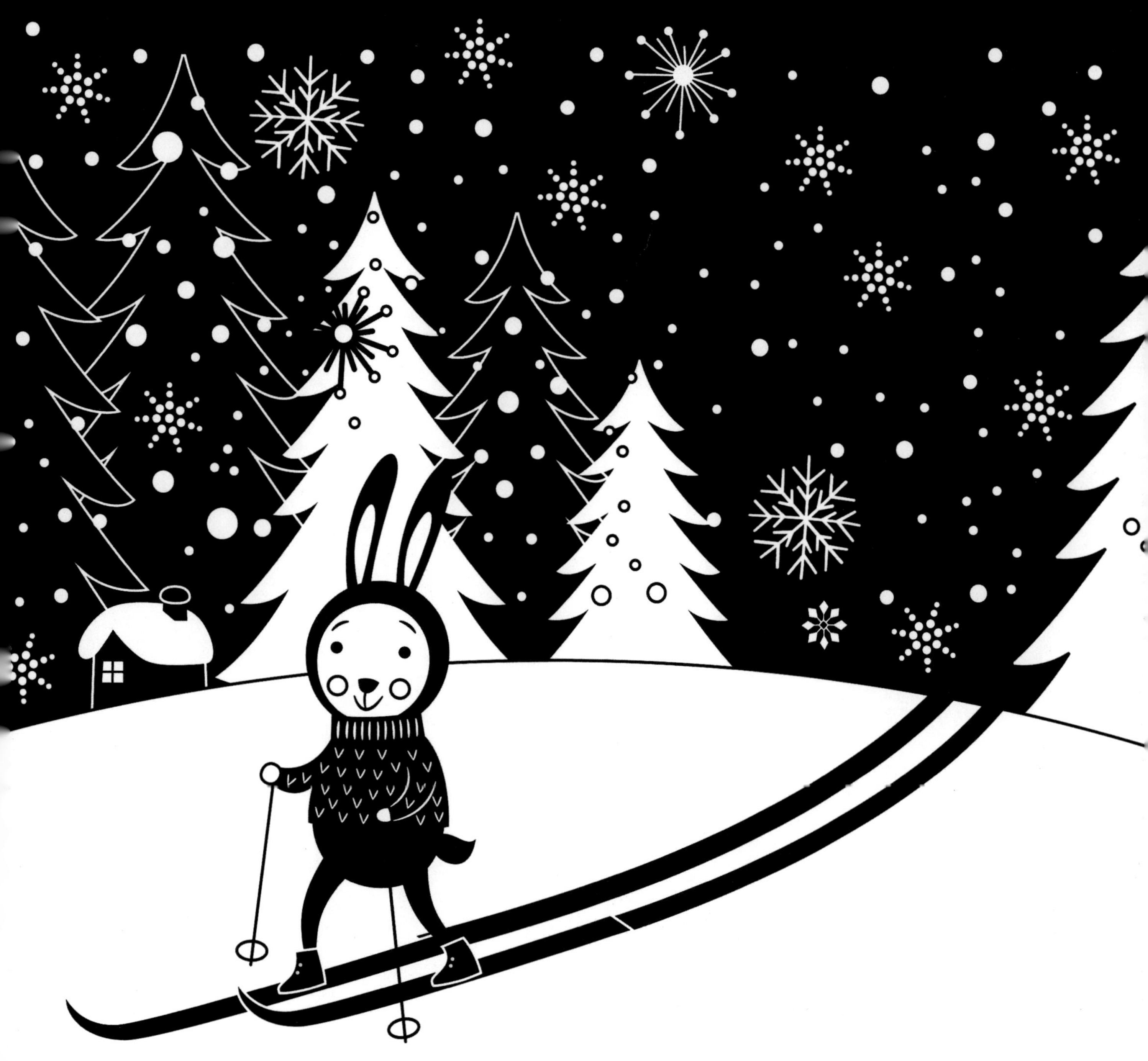

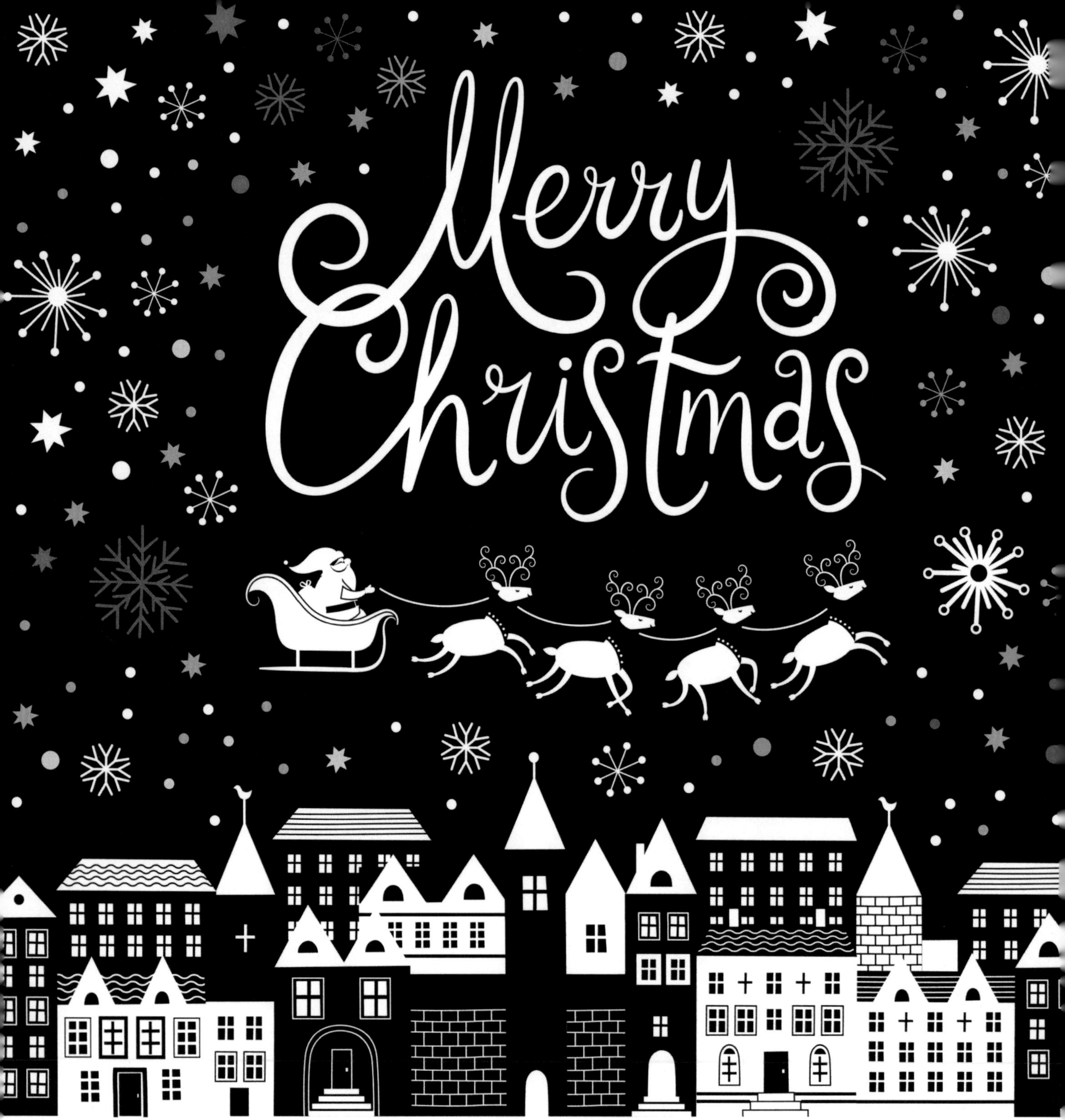
Merry Christmas

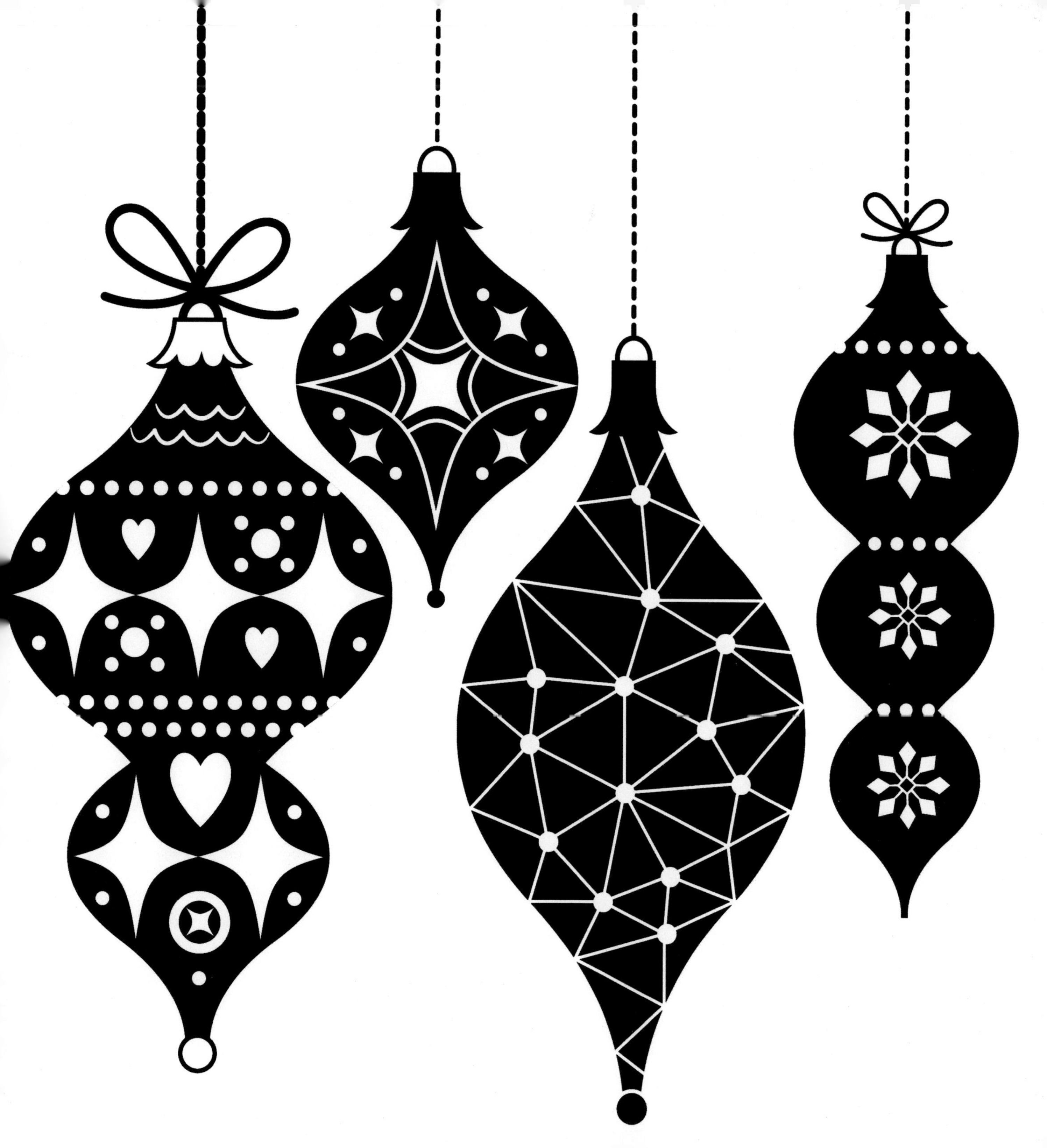

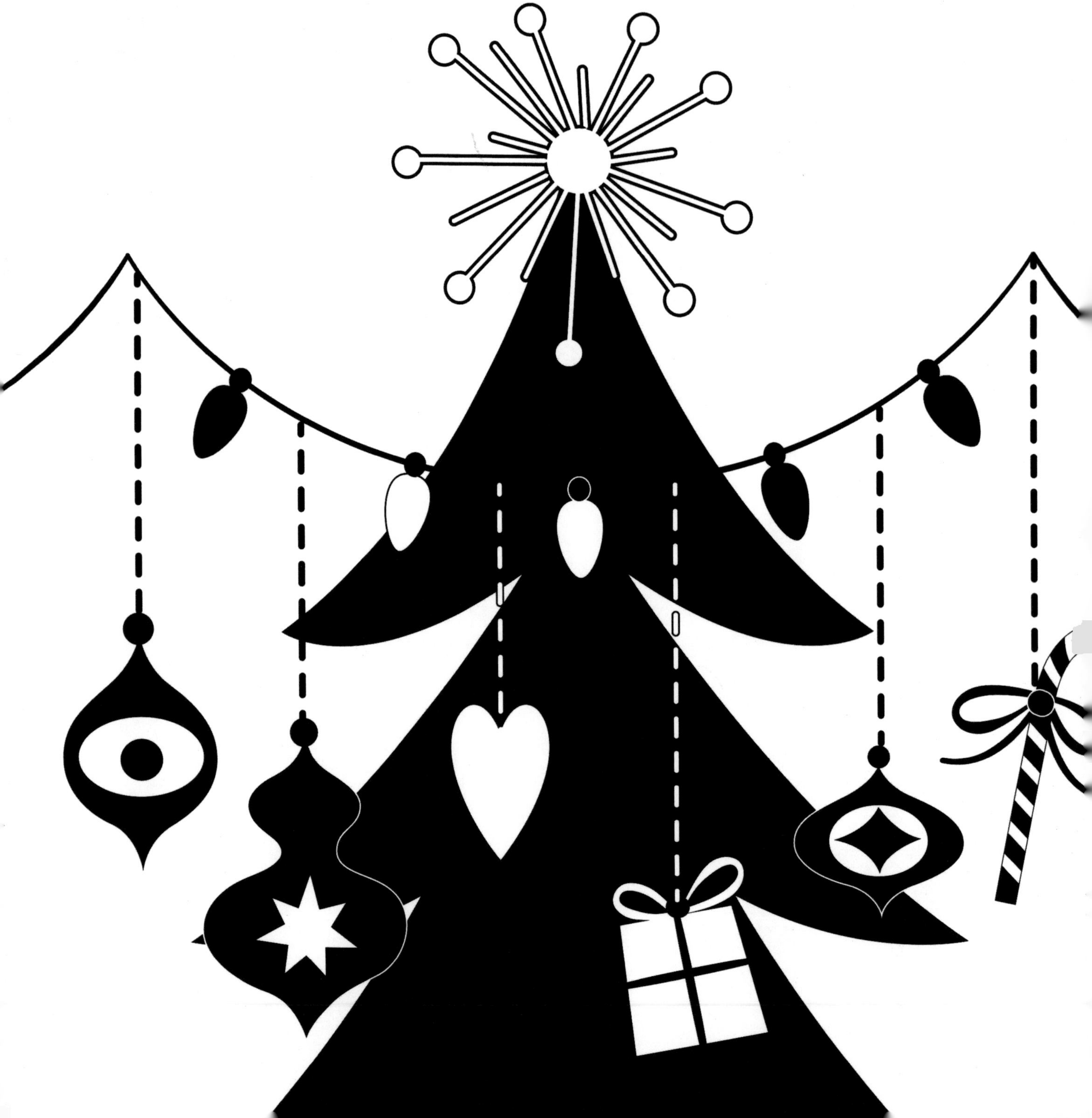

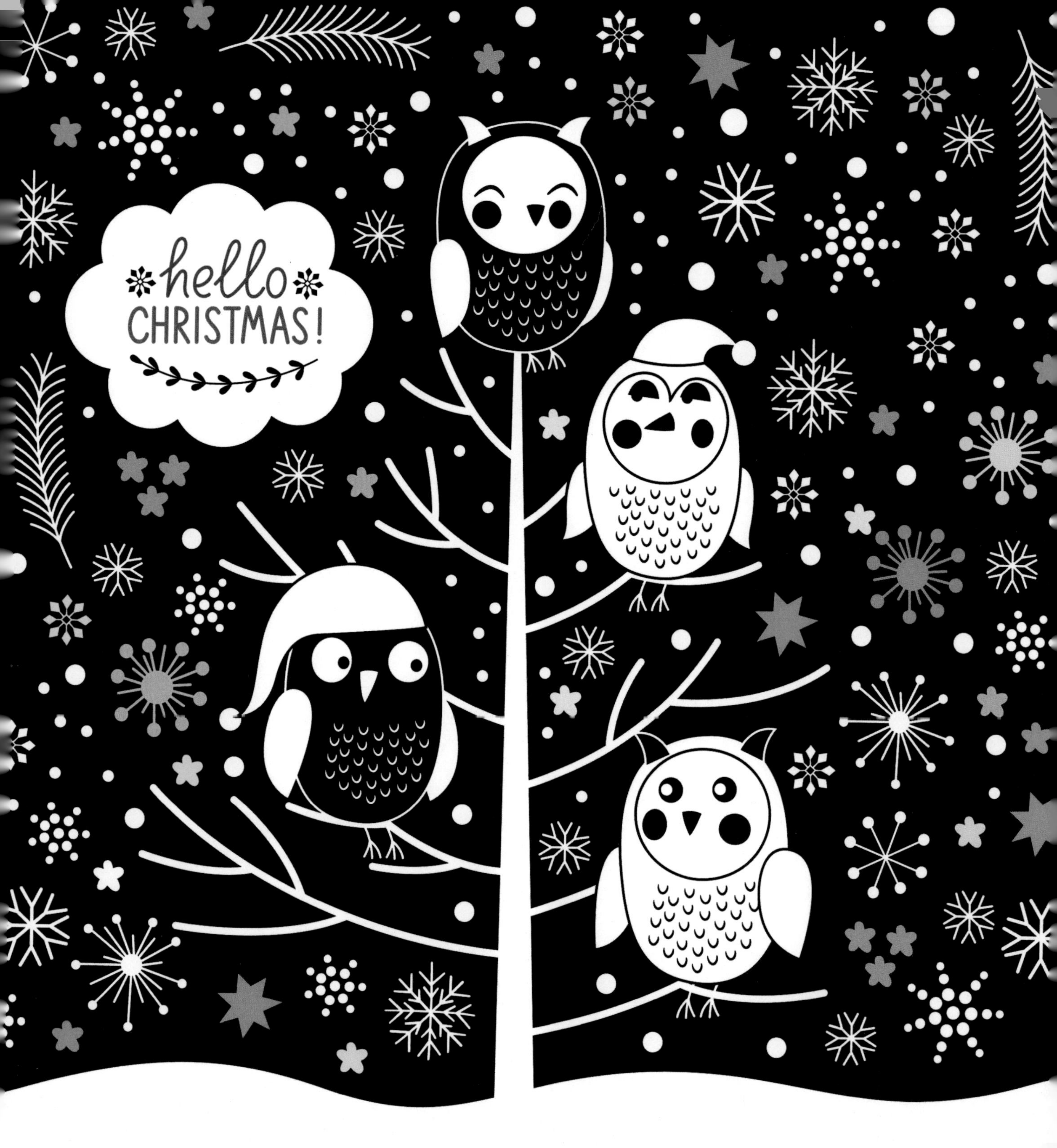
hello
CHRISTMAS!

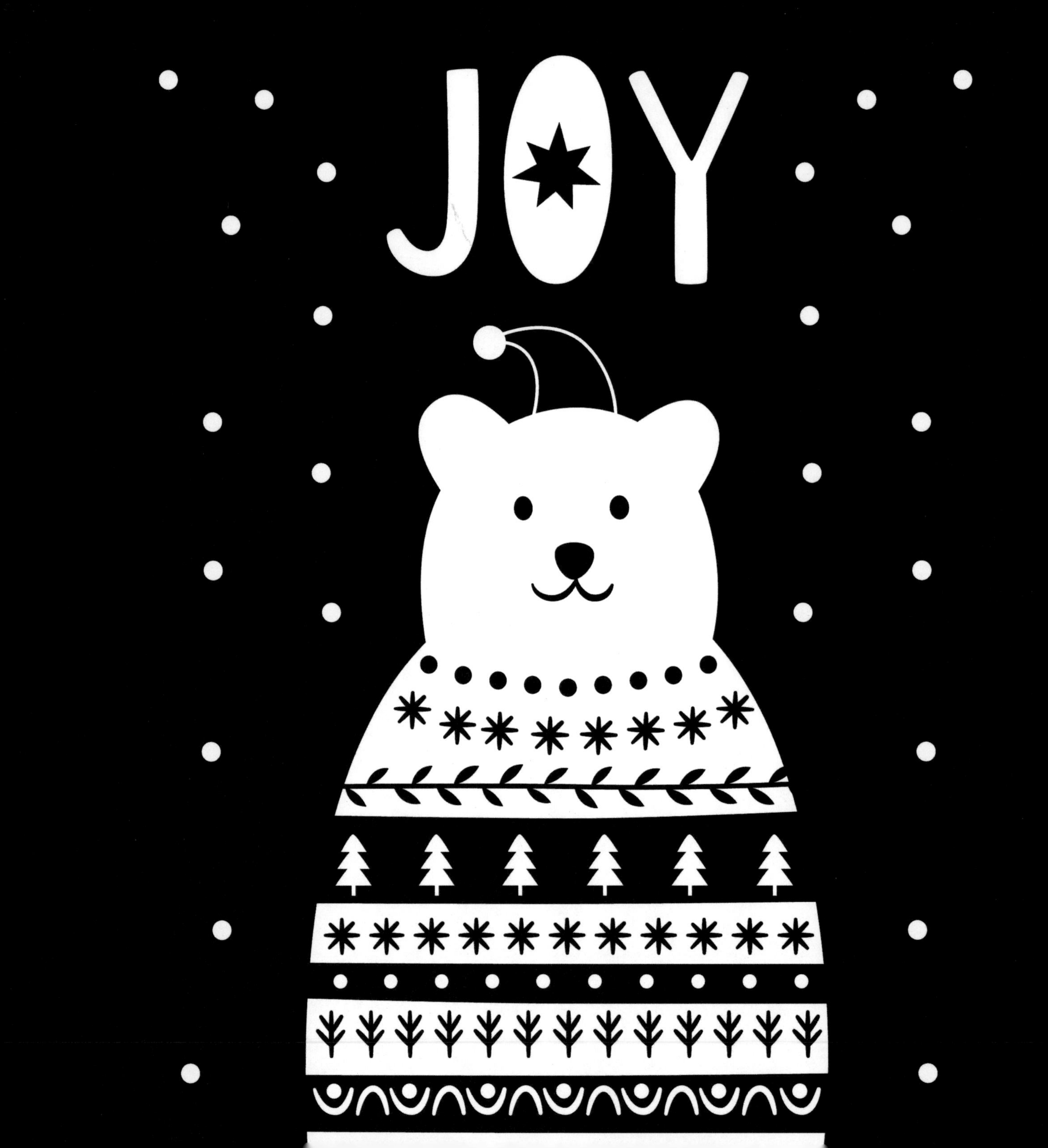
JOY

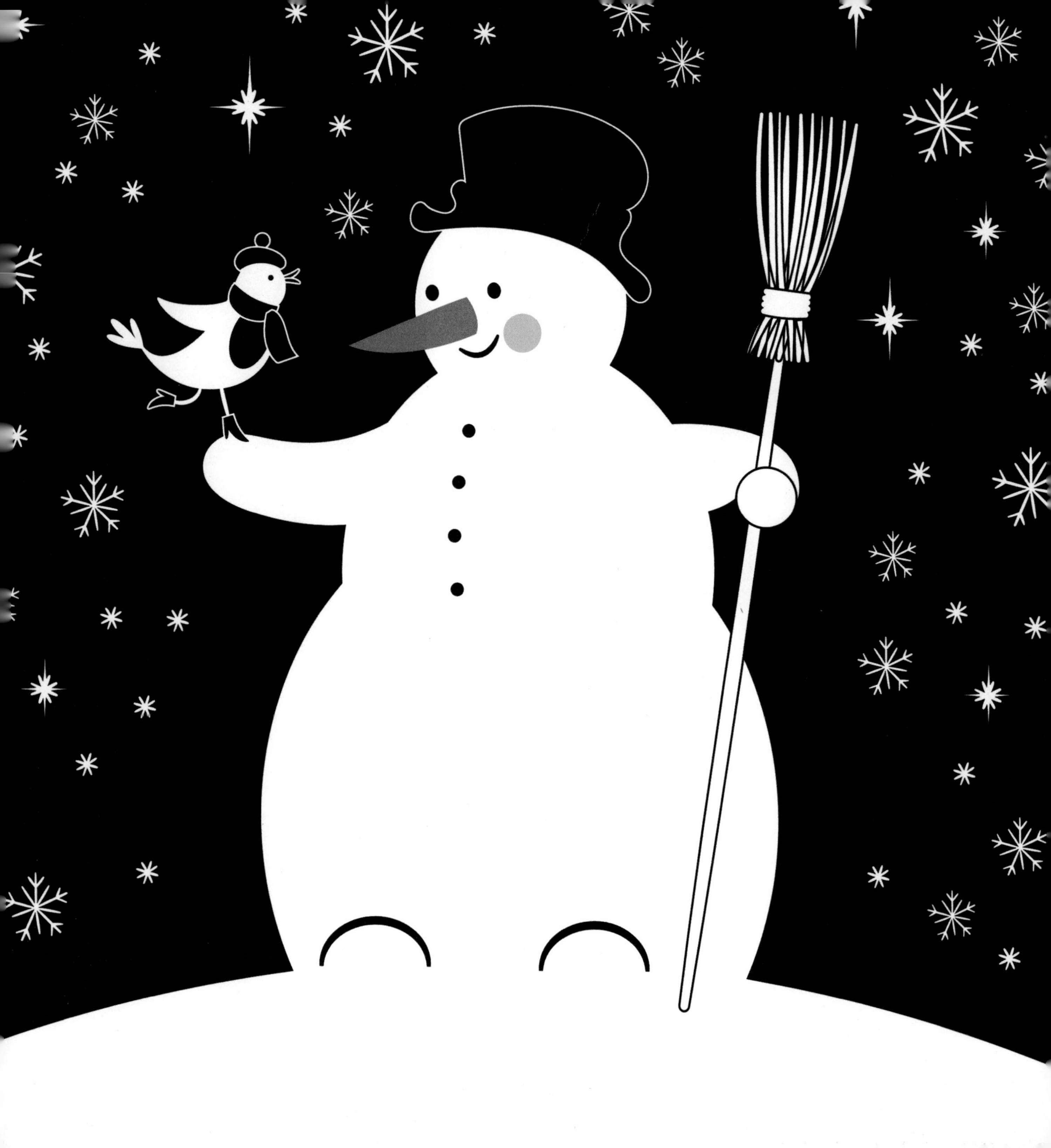

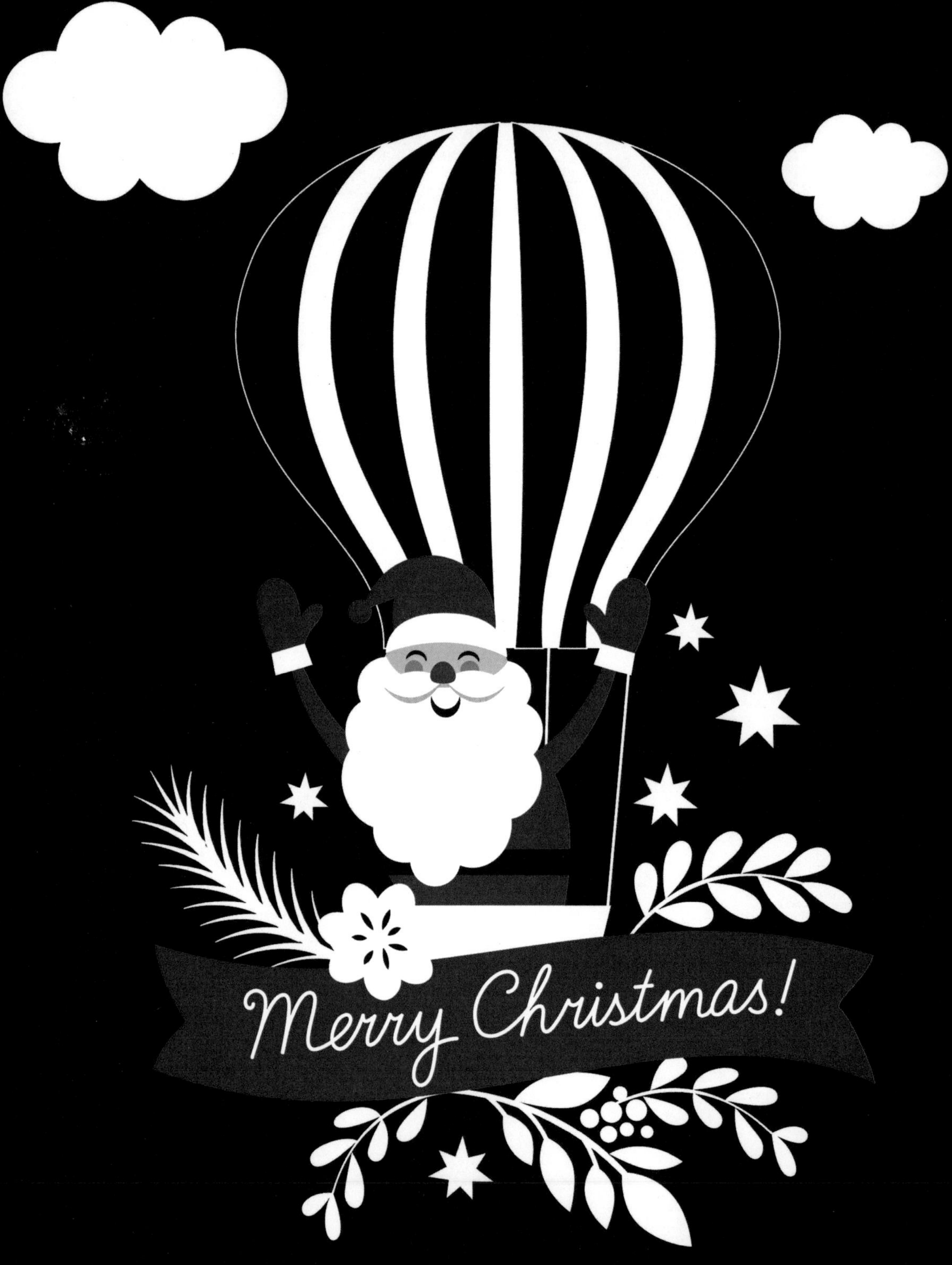
Merry Christmas!

38911450R00015

Made in the USA
Columbia, SC
07 December 2018